ANIMAL ARCHITECTS

BEAVERS

by Karen Latchana Kenney

pogo

Ideas for Parents and Teachers

Pogo Books let children practice reading informational text while introducing them to nonfiction features such as headings, labels, sidebars, maps, and diagrams, as well as a table of contents, glossary, and index.

Carefully leveled text with a strong photo match offers early fluent readers the support they need to succeed.

Before Reading

• "Walk" through the book and point out the various nonfiction features. Ask the student what purpose each feature serves.

• Look at the glossary together. Read and discuss the words.

Read the Book

• Have the child read the book independently.

• Invite him or her to list questions that arise from reading.

After Reading

• Discuss the child's questions. Talk about how he or she might find answers to those questions.

• Prompt the child to think more. Ask: Have you ever seen a beaver dam or another structure made by beavers? Did you see the beavers building it?

Pogo Books are published by Jump!
5357 Penn Avenue South
Minneapolis, MN 55419
www.jumplibrary.com

Library of Congress Cataloging-in-Publication Data

Names: Kenney, Karen Latchana, author.
Title: Beavers / by Karen Latchana Kenney.
Description: Minneapolis, MN: Jump!, Inc., [2017]
Series: Animal architects | Audience: Ages 7-10.
Includes bibliographical references and index.
Identifiers: LCCN 2016048930 (print)
LCCN 2016050344 (ebook)
ISBN 9781620316924 (hardcover: alk. paper)
ISBN 9781624965692 (ebook)
Subjects: LCSH: Beavers–Habitations–
Juvenile literature. | Beavers–Juvenile literature.
Animal behavior–Juvenile literature.
Classification: LCC QL737.R632 K46 2017 (print)
LCC QL737.R632 (ebook) | DDC 599.37156–dc23
LC record available at https://lccn.loc.gov/2016048930

Editor: Kirsten Chang
Book Designer: Michelle Sonnek
Photo Researcher: Michelle Sonnek

Photo Credits: Joel Sartore/Getty, cover, 3; givaga/Shutterstock, cover; Minden Pictures/SuperStock, 1; Kingcraft/Shutterstock, 4; stanley45/iStock, 5; Jody Ann/Shutterstock, 6-7; Michael Francis Photo/age fotostock, 8; Tom & Pat Leeson/Kimball Stock, 9; Robert McGouey/Alamy Stock Photo, 10-11; Rémi Masson/Biosphoto, 12-13; Ilene MacDonald/Alamy Stock Photo, 14-15; Tom & Pat Leeson/age fotostock, 16-17; robert cicchetti/Shutterstock, 18; Cyndi Monaghan/Getty, 19; MeePoohyaPhoto/Shutterstock, 19; Tom & Pat Leeson/Ardea, 20-21; Accent Alaska/Alamy Stock Photo, 23.

Printed in the United States of America at Corporate Graphics in North Mankato, Minnesota.

TABLE OF CONTENTS

CHAPTER 1

GNAWING TREES

Deep in the forest, a beaver gathers wood. It is building a **dam**.

It stands up tall. Its flat tail pushes against the ground. Then it grabs onto a tree.

With its head sideways, it bites. Its teeth scrape the wood. The beaver gnaws halfway through the tree.
Then, crash! The big tree falls.

Beavers are builders. These **mammals** have sharp front teeth. They never stop growing. Beavers use them to cut and gnaw. Their hands can grip and hold sticks, mud, and rocks. Their flat tails and webbed feet make them great swimmers. They need to be strong swimmers to move heavy logs and branches into position.

DID YOU KNOW?

Beavers are **rodents**, like mice or rats. They are the largest rodents in North America.

 tail ·····▶

teeth

webbed
feet

CHAPTER 2

BUSY BUILDERS

Beavers use branches to make a **lodge**. This is a beaver's home.

A growing family lives in a lodge.
The family, or **colony**, is made
of parents and their young.
The youngest beavers are called kits.
Older **offspring** are called yearlings.
Up to eight beavers make a colony.

To make their home, the beavers pile branches in a large **mound**. The sticks lock together, just like a bird's nest. Then the beavers add mud to seal it tight. Inside is a warm, dry room.

DID YOU KNOW?

Beavers eat leaves, bark, twigs, and plants. They store branches and shrubs under their lodge. This is their food all winter long.

Their lodge needs to be surrounded by deep water. Underwater tunnels lead to the doors. This keeps beavers safe from **predators**.

Beavers build long dams to stop streams and rivers. This creates ponds with deep water.

In winter, water flows below the pond's ice. Beavers can still swim to get their food.

TAKE A LOOK!

Where does a beaver keep its food? How does it get into its home? Under the water!

■ = beaver dam   ■ = ice   ■ = beaver lodge
■ = soil   ■ = water   ■ = beaver
                               ■ = beaver food

Beavers dams are wider at the bottom. They get smaller at the top. Dams are mostly made of logs. Rocks hold the logs in place. Twigs, plants, and mud fill in the holes.

Holes and leaks are problems. Beavers stay busy fixing their dams.

beaver dam

Leaky dams need more logs and branches. Hungry beavers need more food, too. They use trees around their ponds first. Then they find them farther away.

Beavers dig long **canals** from their pond. It's easier to move logs and branches in water. Beavers float them back to their pond.

CHAPTER 3

CHANGING THE LAND

Beaver dams make ponds that **flood** the land. The water adds **nutrients** to the soil. They also make a **habitat** for plants and animals.

Lily plants grow in the water. Dragonflies and other **insects** live by the plants. Fish and frogs eat the insects. Birds nest there and eat the insects, too. The ponds become homes to many creatures.

But beaver dams can also cause damage. Dams can stop fish from laying eggs. Ponds can flood nearby roads or bridges. Flooding can hurt and kill trees.

Beavers cutting down trees for their dams causes problems, too. Tree roots keep soil in place by streams. Without trees, the soil washes away.

Look in the forest. You'll find beavers always building. Their dams, lodges, and canals change the land.

BUILD A BEAVER DAM

Build a beaver dam in a box. See what design works best to keep water out.

What You Need:
- plastic box
- sand
- small twigs
- small rocks
- dirt
- water

1. Put sand in the bottom of the box. Fill it up an inch or two (two and a half or five centimeters).

2. Drag your finger along the sand to make a riverbed.

3. Choose a spot and use sticks and rocks to build your dam across the riverbed. Try placing the sticks and rocks different ways. Which design do you think will work best?

4. Make some mud with the dirt and water. Stick it onto the sides of your dam.

5. Slowly pour water into the riverbed. Did your dam work? If not, try another design.

canals: Channels dug out of land that fill with water from a pond or lake.

colony: A beaver family group that lives together.

dam: A strong barrier built across rivers or streams that blocks water.

flood: To cover or become filled with a great flow of water.

habitat: The natural home of a plant or animal.

insects: Small animals with six legs and three body parts.

lodge: A home built with sticks and mud where beavers live.

mammals: Warm-blooded animals that have fur or hair and a spine.

mound: A hill or pile.

nutrients: Substances that are essential for living things to survive and grow.

offspring: An animal's young.

predators: Animals that hunt and eat other animals.

rodents: Mammals with large front teeth used to gnaw things.

TO LEARN MORE

Learning more is as easy as 1, 2, 3.

1) Go to www.factsurfer.com

2) Enter "beaverarchitects" into the search box.

3) Click the "Surf" button to see a list of websites.

With factsurfer, finding more information is just a click away.